Best Breakfast Sandwich Maker Recipes

Easy Homemade Sandwich for Beginners

Heidi Chen

This is a collection of 55 delicious sandwich recipes for brunch, breakfast, lunch, dinner, snack or a meal. In this cookbook you'll discover our secrets with step-by-step recipes for all of their most beloved specialties. You will discover how to create new varieties of very delicious sandwiches for you and your family.

Table of content

AVOCADO SANDWICH

for 4 people INGREDIENTS

- 2 ripe avocados

- 4 "pita" bread rolls

- 100 g finely chopped shallot

- 2 peeled tomatoes with seeds removed and coarsely chopped

- 3 tablespoons of lemon juice

- 1 tablespoon of coriander

- 1/2 teaspoon of chili powder

- Tabasco lettuce leaves

- salt, pepper

PREPARATION

Peel the avocados, remove the stone and mash the pulp; add the shallot, lemon juice, chili, tomato, coriander, tabasco, salt, and pepper as required. Finally, mix well until you get a thick cream. Now cut the sandwiches in half, put a lettuce leaf in the center, and spread the previously prepared mixture over it. Serve immediately.

BRAZILIAN SANDWICH

for 4 people INGREDIENTS

- 3 bananas
- 150 g of very lean cooked ham
- 2 stalks of very white celery
- 8 slices of sandwich bread
- 1 onion - 1 tablespoon of Dijon mustard
- 2-3 tablespoons of butter

PREPARATION

Cut the ham into small pieces, chop the celery and onion, cut the banana and mix everything in the food processor to obtain a homogeneous puree. Now work the butter with the mustard and spread it on the four slices of bread. Then take the mixture obtained from the banana and distribute it over the sandwich, now recompose the sandwich with the other slices of bread and serve it.

MIXED MEAT SANDWICH

for 4 people INGREDIENTS

- 12 slices of sandwich bread

- 200 g of meat, chicken or turkey cooked thinly sliced

- 3 firm and ripe tomatoes sliced and without seeds

- 4 slices of cooked ham

- butter 1/2 liter of mayonnaise

- 1/2 teaspoon of Dijon mustard

- lettuce leaves

- 8 strips of crispy fried bacon

- 4 large black or green olives

PREPARATION

Toast 8 slices of bread, take four and use them as a base for sandwiches. Mix the mayonnaise with the mustard. On the base put a slice of chicken with mayonnaise, a little lettuce, a slice of tomato and a strip of bacon, now overlap a slice of buttered bread with a little mayonnaise and add another slice of cooked ham, a slice of tomato, one of bacon; finally cover everything with another toasted slice. Do the same with the other slices of bread. Decorate the sandwiches with a toothpick and an olive.

VEGETABLE SANDWICH

for 6 people INGREDIENTS

- 6 slices of bread
- 80 g of chopped cabbage
- 80 g of chopped carrots
- 50 g of chopped green pepper
- 50 g of chopped celery
- 50 g of chopped radishes
- 100 g of chopped sweet onion
- 400 g of grated Parmesan cheese
- 1/2 cup of beer
- butter
- White pepper
- cayenne
- pepper
- salt

PREPARATION

Take a bowl and put the carrots, pepper, celery, radishes, cabbage and onion in it, season with salt and mix well. Meanwhile, toast the slices of bread and, as soon as they are ready, spread the butter on them and place the vegetable mixture on them.

Put the tomato sauce and cheese in a separate pan, cook until you get a thick and homogeneous sauce. Now take a saucepan and sprinkle it with butter, take the slices of bread and put them in the casserole, put the cheese sauce on top and simmer them for 3 minutes until the cheese has melted on the slices. Serve.

TOMATO SANDWICH

for 3 or 6 people INGREDIENTS

- large tomatoes
- 180 g of soft white cheese like Philadelphia
- 2 tablespoons of cream
- 1 clove of garlic
- 1 egg - 120 g of breadcrumbs
- 2 tablespoons of butter - salt

PREPARATION

Cut 12 slices of tomato about 1 centimeter thick, spread them on absorbent paper and let them dry for five minutes. Take a bowl and put the cheese, chopped garlic, cream and mix well until you get a homogeneous mixture. Now spread 6 tomato slices with the mixture and place the other tomato slice on top of each slice. Beat an egg and dip the tomato sandwiches in it, dip them in the breadcrumbs, do it with the rest of the tomato sandwiches. Take a pan and butter it, dip the tomato sandwiches and cook for about 3 minutes until golden brown. Finally, place them on a serving dish and put a pinch of salt in them. Now serve.

POTATO SANDWICH

for 4 people INGREDIENTS

- 1 kg of potatoes
- 100 g of butter - 200 g of sliced cooked ham
- 100 g of grated Emmental
- other cheese cut into thin slices - 2 eggs, flour, salt

PREPARATION

After having peeled the potatoes, boil them in salted water and as soon as they are ready, mash them until a homogeneous puree is obtained. Now take a pastry board and flour it, put the mashed potatoes and add a knob of butter, the eggs and mix well, finally level the puree mixture to a thickness of one centimeter, flour it and let it rest for about 30 minutes. When the mashed potatoes have cooled and are more compact, cut them into rectangles.

Then take a pan and sprinkle it with butter, as soon as it is hot put the crushed balls in it until the pan is full, then put on each rectangle half a slice of ham and the cheese cut into rectangles of the same shape as the puree, to finish cover all the rectangles of the pan well.

Now take a saucepan from the oven and butter it, then put in the loaves that were in the pan. Cover with grated Emmental and butter flakes and bake in the oven at 180° for about half an hour. Finally, arrange the sandwiches on a serving dish and serve.

EGGPLANT SANDWICH

for 4 people INGREDIENTS

- 3 aubergines
- tomato sauce made with 1/2 kg of tomatoes
- basil, garlic, onion, oil
- 150 g of thin slices of cheese
- 2 eggs - flour breadcrumbs
- oil for frying - salt

PREPARATION

Slice the aubergines and sprinkle them with salt so that they lose excess water. Now take a slice of aubergine and spread the tomato sauce over it and close it with another slice of aubergine, pass the sandwich in the flour, then in the egg, and then in the breadcrumbs. Finally, prepare the rest of the aubergines in the same way and fry them in a pan with hot oil until cooked. As soon as the eggplant sandwiches are ready, drain them with absorbent paper. To serve.

MUSHROOMS SANDWICH

for 4 people INGREDIENTS

- 16 medium sized porcini mushrooms
- 200 g of roasted meat leftovers
- 90 g of lard
- 30 g of butter
- 1 stale milk sandwich
- 3 eggs
- 50 g of grated Parmesan cheese
- milk
- breadcrumbs
- flour
- parsley
- salt

PREPARATION

Clean the mushrooms, remove the stems and chop them in half, because we will use them for two different dishes. Brown the mushrooms in a pan with 30 grams of lard and butter for about 12 minutes. Meanwhile pass the meat with the food processor. Take a bowl and pour in the breadcrumbs, milk, mushroom stem, minced meat, chopped parsley, an egg and grated Parmesan. At this point season the mushroom-shaped chapels with a pinch of salt and spread the previously worked mixture on them, then pass them in the flour, then in the beaten eggs and again in the breadcrumbs.

Put them to cook in the lard, turning them often and browning them until they become golden and crunchy. As soon as the mushrooms are cooked, let them drain for a few minutes in the absorbent paper.

Now put them on a serving dish and serve hot.

for 6 people INGREDIENTS - 2 cucumbers

- 1 teaspoon of white vinegar
- 1/2 teaspoon of salt
- 6 very thin slices of dark bread
- butter

PREPARATION

Cut 40 discs of very thin cucumbers, mix them with the vinegar and let them rest for 30 minutes so that they lose their water.

With a mold, cut four discs from the slices of bread and spread a layer of butter on them. Season the bread with the cucumber discs and cover them with the other half. As soon as they are ready, put them in the fridge to rest for 30 minutes covered with a damp cloth. Finally arrange them on a serving dish and serve.

SANDWICH WITH MEATBALLS

for 4 people INGREDIENTS

- 4 "pita" sandwiches
- 200 g of naturally boiled chickpeas
- 4 pinches of coriander
- 4 pinches of cumin
- 2 cloves of garlic
- 8 lettuce leaves
- 3-4 ripe tomatoes
- 3 tablespoons of tahini (sesame seed paste)
- 1 tablespoon of sesame seeds
- parsley
- 1/2 teaspoon of paprika
- 1 red pepper
- 1 tablespoon of lemon juice
- flour
- oil for frying
- cayenne pepper
- salt

PREPARATION

Start with preparing the meatballs. Take a food processor
and blend the chickpeas, place them in a bowl and toss

with the cumin, finely chopped garlic, coriander and salt and cayenne pepper. As soon as the mixture is ready, let it rest for 30 minutes, prepare the meatballs, mash them and cover with flour.

Now prepare the sauce with the tahini, parsley, lemon juice, a finely chopped clove of garlic, paprika, a pinch of salt and mix. At this point, fry the meatballs in oil and drain them in absorbent paper. Remove the breadcrumbs and stuff them with a lettuce leaf, sliced pepper and tomato. Now season the meatballs with the tahini sauce and place them in the center of the sandwich. Serve.

VEGETARIAN SANDWICH

for 8 people INGREDIENTS

- 8 milk rolls
- 2 hard boiled eggs
- 1 fennel
- 2 tomatoes
- 2 layers of green pepper in oil
- 2 sticks of celery
- 130 g of tuna in oil
- 8 anchovies stuffed with capers
- 8 olives stuffed with peppers
- 1 tablespoon of mayonnaise
- 1 pack of white yogurt
- 1 teaspoon of Worcestershire sauce
- chives
- salt and pepper

PREPARATION

Cut the sandwiches in half and remove the crumb. Now cut the pepper, the fennel and chop the tomato with the celery. Meanwhile, drain the tuna and mix all the ingredients in a bowl.

Fill the sandwiches with this topping. In another bowl pour the Worcestershire sauce, yogurt, and chives, mix everything, then season with salt and pepper.

Then garnish the top of the sandwiches with a wedge of hard-boiled egg, an olive, and capers.

Finally, put the sauce made with yogurt in a separate bowl and serve the sandwiches on a serving dish.

for 4 people INGREDIENTS
- 8 milk sandwiches - 4 eggs
- 150 g of champignons - 1 shallot
- 50 g of butter
- 3 tablespoons of cream
- 1 tablespoon of tomato sauce
- Tabasco
- salt
- pepper

PREPARATION

Cut the mushrooms and chop them, then take a pan and put 20 grams of butter in it, add the shallot and brown. While cooking, season with salt and pepper and cook for about 12 minutes, add a few drops of Tabasco and tomato.

In the meantime, cut the sandwiches in two and brush the inside with butter, then place them in the oven to lightly toast at 175 degrees.

Now beat the eggs with the cream, then season with salt and pepper, now add the mixture that you had previously prepared.

Finally, take the sandwiches out of the oven, take the mixture obtained and distribute it inside the sandwiches, close with the other half and serve.

MEDITERRANEAN SANDWICH

for 6 people INGREDIENTS

- 1 narrow loaf or 1 baguette
- 400 g of coarsely chopped tomato pulp
- 100 g of thinly sliced shallot
- 50 g of green olives stuffed with pepper, chopped
- 50 g of pitted and chopped black olives
- 30 g of chopped parsley
- 1 teaspoon of chopped fresh thyme or 1 pinch of dried one
- 1 tablespoon of capers
- 1 tablespoon of chopped basil
- 2-3 tablespoons of olive oil - salt, pepper

PREPARATION

Remove the two ends from the loaf by cutting them with a knife and remove the crumb inside them, chop the remaining excess crumb with a food processor.

Take a large bowl and mix the tomato, black olives, capers, green olives, basil, thyme, parsley, shallot, and the crumb, now add the oil to soften the mixture, finally salt and pepper. just enough.

As soon as the mixture is ready, fill the loaf and wrap it in aluminum foil and put it in the fridge for at least seven hours or overnight. Before serving, take it out of the fridge at least an hour before, slice and distribute the sandwiches.

for 8 people INGREDIENTS

- 8 milk rolls
- 130 g Russian salad
- 2 tablespoons of mayonnaise
- 8 small lettuce leaves

PREPARATION

Wash the lettuce and dry it.

Take the sandwiches and split them in half, immediately spread the mayonnaise on both sides and put a lettuce leaf inside them, then take the Russian salad and put it in the middle. Finally, lightly press the sandwiches and serve.

MIXED VEGETABLE SANDWICH

for 4 people INGREDIENTS

- 4 sandwiches

- 70 g of butter

- 2 carrots

- 2-3 courgettes

- 2 handfuls of peas

- 1 cup of broth

PREPARATION

Cut the sandwiches in two and remove the crumb. Put the vegetables in a pan and boil for a few minutes, as soon as the water starts to evaporate, put the butter in the pan and brown the vegetables. Spread the butter inside the sandwiches and add the browned vegetables. Now take a pan, dust it with butter and place the sandwiches on the bottom, pour the broth over it and sprinkle it on the sandwiches, now wait for them to become crispy. When the sandwiches are ready, place them on a serving dish and serve.

AGRO SANDWICH

for 4 people INGREDIENTS

- 4 slices of bread
- green salad
- 70 g of butter
- parsley
- the juice of 1 lemon, salt

PREPARATION

Take a cup of milk and add the lemon juice, parsley, butter and mix everything until you get a homogeneous mixture. Meanwhile, toast the slices of bread in the oven for 6/7 minutes, as soon as they come out of the oven spread a layer of butter and immediately add the mixture with the lemon, now garnish the slice of bread with the green salad and serve.

CARRETERA SANDWICH

for 4 people INGREDIENTS

- 4 sandwiches
- fresh tomatoes
- garlic, chopped basil
- oil, salt, pepper

PREPARATION

Cut the sandwiches in half, then put them to toast for a few minutes. Meanwhile, chop the tomatoes and mix with oil, pepper, salt, basil and garlic, mix everything with a wooden spoon and season while still hot, remember to remove the garlic. Before closing the sandwich with the other half you can still add a drizzle of oil, salt and pepper to flavor the top of the sandwich. Arrange the sandwiches on a serving dish and serve immediately.

PAN BAGNAT NIZZA

for 4 people INGREDIENTS

- 4 large slices of stale Tuscan or Apulian homemade bread
- 4 ripe and firm tomatoes
- 2 tablespoons of vinegar
- 2 tablespoons of virgin olive oil - lettuce leaves - black olives

onion rings - fresh basil - salt and pepper

PREPARATION

Fill a glass of cold water, place the slices of bread on a large plate, wet them and let them rest for about 20 minutes until the water is absorbed by the slices of bread. After 20 minutes, remove the excess water, but be careful that the slices remain intact. Now take a serving dish and spread out the slices of bread, then put a lettuce leaf on top, the sliced tomato and season with oil, salt and vinegar. Before serving, garnish with black olives, onion, basil leaves and leave to rest for 15 minutes before serving.

TOMATO SANDWICH

for 4 people INGREDIENTS

- 4 slices of homemade bread
- 4 thick slices of ripe tomatoes
- 4 thin slices of fontina
- butter
- mayonnaise
- Dijon mustard

PREPARATION

After toasting the slices of bread on one side only, spread the untoasted side with the butter, mustard and mayonnaise. Finally add a slice of cheese and a slice of tomato. Then grill it until the cheese has melted or turns slightly golden. Then serve.

BLACK OLIVE CROUTONS

for 10 people INGREDIENTS

- 10 round rolls

- 150 g of pitted and chopped black olives

- 100 g of mayonnaise

- 2 tablespoons of finely chopped onion

- 150 g of grated Gruyere cheese

- 1/2 teaspoon of curry powder

PREPARATION

Take the sandwiches, cut them in two and toast them. Then take a bowl where you will go to work the mayonnaise, olives, onion, curry and cheese. Take the sandwiches and divide the mixture obtained previously and sprinkle it on the toasted sandwiches, then place them on the grill and cook for about 4 minutes. finally take a serving dish and arrange the sandwiches before serving.

MUSHROOM CROUTONS

for 4 people INGREDIENTS

- 1/2 kg of thinly sliced cultivated mushrooms
- 4 slices of homemade bread
- 3 and a half tablespoons of butter
- 2 tablespoons of flour 3.5 dl of milk
- 1.5 dl of dry white wine
- 4 teaspoons of finely chopped onion
- 1 tablespoon of soy sauce
- 2 tablespoons of brandy grated parmesan
- salt
- pepper

PREPARATION

Take a medium-sized pan and melt a tablespoon of butter, add the flour and cook over low heat for about 4 minutes. Meanwhile, stir slowly and add the milk and the wine, mix it slowly with a ladle and wait for the sauce to thicken, season with salt and pepper, then cook for another 14 minutes.

Take another pan and sprinkle it with butter, let it heat up, add the mushrooms and let them brown for about 3 minutes.

Now take the heated brandy, set the pan on fire until the flames have gone out.

Place the four slices of bread in the bowls and pour the mushrooms over them, then sprinkle with the sauce and grated Parmesan.

Cook everything at 200° for about 10 minutes waiting for the cheese to melt and turn slightly golden. Serve.

TUNA AND ROASTED PEPPER SANDWICH

for 6 people INGREDIENTS

- 1 large flat bread with thyme or rosemary or
- 6 rolls of Arab bread
- 200 g tuna in oil
- 3 large peeled roasted red peppers
- 2 tablespoons of lemon juice
- 1 teaspoon of finely chopped fresh thyme
- 50 ml plus 2 tablespoons of extra virgin olive oil
- 120 g of parsley leaves1 thinly sliced red onion
- 2 tablespoons of capers salt and pepper

PREPARATION

Drain the tuna and put it in a bowl with a little lemon juice, onion, thyme, salt and pepper as required. Take another bowl and put the remaining tuna with oil, parsley and always season with salt and pepper.

At this point, cut the focaccia in half and fill it with the slices of roasted pepper and the mixture obtained previously. Finally, cover the focaccia with the other half and put it in the fridge covered with plastic wrap for about 50 minutes. Before serving, cut it into wedges.

OYSTER SANDWICH

for 4 people INGREDIENTS

- 8 very thin slices of whole grain bread
- 8 large oysters
- 2 tablespoons of mustard
- 1 tablespoon of ketchup sauce
- 40 g of butter
- lemon
- parsley
- salt and pepper

PREPARATION

Open the oysters and place them in a container, keeping the liquid. Take a bowl and work the butter together with a sprinkling of ground pepper, a pinch of salt and finally add a few drops of oyster liquid, then mix until you get a creamy mixture. Prepare the slices of bread and spread the butter on them, take the oysters with a spoon and put them on all four slices of bread, add the parsley and a squeeze of lemon. Finally, make a mixture of butter, hot sauce, and mustard to garnish the sandwich. Put the sandwiches obtained in the fridge until you serve them.

SARDINES SANDWICH

for 4 people INGREDIENTS

- 8 slices of bread100 g of butter
- 1 tablespoon of anchovy paste
- 100 g of tuna in oil
- 1 tin of sardines without bones
- parsley, chopped onion

PREPARATION

Take the tuna and crumble it, then add the butter with the anchovy paste, the sardines, the parsley. finely chopped onion and mix until a consistent mixture is obtained. Finally spread the slices of bread with the creamy mixture and cover them with the other slices. Serve on a serving plate.

DANISH SANDWICH

for 6 people INGREDIENTS

- 6 slices of sandwich bread
- 250 g cooked lobster, crab or shrimp pulp
- 1 small jar of black or red caviar
- 3 hard-boiled eggs
- 6 lettuce leaves
- 1 tablespoon of mayonnaise
- a pinch of mustard powder
- butter to garnish: tomato wedges - parsley sprigs - lemon wedges

PREPARATION

After having properly toasted the slices of bread, spread the butter on one side. Add a lettuce leaf and with a spoon pour the shellfish pulp on the slices and add a spoonful of black caviar. Meanwhile, cut the eggs into two parts and remove the yolk. Take a bowl and put the mustard with the mayonnaise and add the previously removed yolk and mix until you get a creamy mixture. Now fill the half eggs with the mixture obtained. Finally, put the half egg in the center of the caviar with the addition of parsley. Arrange the sandwiches on a serving dish and garnish with pieces of tomato, lemon, and parsley sprigs.

STURGEON SANDWICH

for 4 people INGREDIENTS

- 8 very thin slices of rye bread
- 4 slices of smoked sturgeon
- 4 teaspoons of caviar or lumpfish egg
- butter
- fresh chive strands
- lemon
- pepper

PREPARATION

Take a plate with the highest edges, now take the sturgeon slices and sprinkle them with lemon juice, season with freshly ground pepper and leave to flavor for about 50 minutes. After draining the sturgeon, take the slices of bread and arrange it on a serving dish and arrange the sturgeon on each slice, lightly butter and add a spoonful of caviar and chives. Close the four slices of bread with the remaining slices. Serve.

ANCHOVIES SANDWICH

for 4 people INGREDIENTS

- 4 sandwiches

- 50 g of butter

- 100 g anchovies fillets

- pepper

- capers

PREPARATION

Take a mortar and prepare the anchovies by working them with 80 grams of anchovies and butter, also add the pepper. In the meantime, remove the crumbs from the sandwiches and spread the anchovies prepared with a mortar on top. Arrange the sandwiches on a serving dish and add a rolled fillet to each sandwich, finally add the capers. Serve.

LOBSTER SANDWICH

for 4 people INGREDIENTS

- 4 sandwiches
- 50 g of butter
- 50 g of grated cheese
- 2 hard-boiled egg yolks
- 1 tablespoon of mustard
- pieces of boiled lobster
- salt

PREPARATION

Take a bowl and melt the cheese, butter and crumbled egg yolks in it until you get a creamy and homogeneous compost.

Then add the mustard, adjusting the mixture with a pinch of salt and mix slowly. In the meantime, open the sandwiches in two parts and spread the cream you just prepared, add pieces of boiled lobster. Serve.

SMOKED SALMON SANDWICH

for 4 people INGREDIENTS

- 8 slices of bread
- 80 g smoked salmon cut into slices
- 40 g of butter
- lemon juice
- 4 lemon slices, peeled and cut into triangles
- freshly ground pepper

PREPARATION

Take the sandwiches and remove the crust, then mix the butter and a little lemon juice. Now spread the mixture obtained previously and spread it on the four slices of bread, then cover the bread with the slices of salmon and add a little lemon pulp and spices to your liking. Serve

CAVIAR SANDWICH

for 4 people INGREDIENTS

- 4 slices of bread in a box
- 200 g of butter
- 1 hard-boiled egg
- 1/2 grated onion
- 1 jar of caviar

PREPARATION

Take the sandwiches and divide them in half and spread the butter on the bottom of the sandwich. Take the hard-boiled egg and put it together with the grated onion on the sandwich, then add a spoonful of caviar. served.

CAVIAR BUTTER SANDWICH

for 4 people INGREDIENTS

- 1 sandwich sliced loaf pan 1/2

- 100 g. butter

- 100 g of caviar

- lemon slices

PREPARATION

Cut the sandwiches and remove the crust, then divide them into triangles. Pass the butter with the caviar in a pan to obtain a tasty homogeneous cream. Then spread the cream on the slices of bread and season to your liking.

SEAFOOD SANDWICH

for 4 people INGREDIENTS

- 4 milk sandwiches
- 8 lettuce leaves
- 2 thinly sliced spring onions
- 3 finely chopped garlic cloves
- 2 teaspoons of curry
- 3 tablespoons of lemon juice
- 2 and 1/2 tablespoons of extra virgin olive oil
- 2 tablespoons of sauce Aurora
- fresh thyme
- 150 g of shrimp
- 150 g of cuttlefish
- 800 g of mussels
- 50 ml of brandy salt and pepper

PREPARATION

Wash the mussels and cuttlefish leaving them immersed in salted water for half an hour. Shell the prawns. After letting the mussels rest in plenty of salted water, put them in a pan with lemon juice and oil, and brown them until their shells open. Then fry the onions with a little garlic and brown the shrimp and cuttlefish, then add the brandy and cook for another 5/6 minutes. Then take the mussels with the sauce you prepared earlier and add the thyme leaves and curry, continue to cook for another 5 minutes.

Finally, cut the salad into small pieces and pour the remaining lemon juice and oil over it, so as to mix the mixture.

Now cut the sandwiches in half and fill them. Serve immediately.

SARDINES AND GROVIERA (CHEES) SANDWICH

for 4 people INGREDIENTS

- 4 sandwiches

- 150 g of canned sardines in oil

- 4 rosettes

- 75 g grated gruyere

- 120 ml white wine vinegar

- 1 small onion, thinly sliced

PREPARATION

Take three ice cubes and put them in a bowl with the onions and add the vinegar, then leave to act for about 15 minutes. Drain the sardines, but be careful to keep the oil. Now remove the crumb at the top of the sandwich. Then take the sandwich, fill it with sardines and add a drizzle of oil. Bring the oven to 200° and bake the sandwiches, but first add a slice of cheese and let it cook for 5 minutes until the cheese has melted. Finally, as soon as the sandwiches are ready, place them on a well heated plate, add the onion rings on top and serve immediately.

SAN JUAN SANDWICH

for 4 people INGREDIENTS

- 4 round rolls (sandwiches) - 1 box of crabmeat
- 40 g of chopped celery
- 40 g of chopped cucumbers
- 1 boiled egg
- 1 finely chopped shallot
- 60 g mayonnaise
- 1 large tomato
- 4 slices of savory cheese - paprika, chopped parsley

PREPARATION

Take the sandwiches, cut them in half and toast them. Then drain the crab meat and clean it of cartilage residues. Cut the sandwiches into slices and toast them in the oven. Meanwhile, mix the crab meat with the cucumber, egg, celery, mayonnaise and shallot. Now cut the tomato into slices and arrange them in the four halves of the sandwich, then take the crab meat with a spoon and distribute it on the tomato slice, add a slice of cheese and a pinch of paprika.

Finally, grill half of the sandwich with the mixture. When

cooked, recompose the sandwich with the other half and serve..

CAVIAR AND VODKA SANDWICH

for 4 people INGREDIENTS

- 4 sandwiches

- 100 g of caviar

- 100 g of butter

- 15 anchovy fillets

- 1 tablespoon of vodka

PREPARATION

Take the anchovy fillets, and after removing the bones, put them in a mortar and mash them. Then prepare the butter making it creamier and add the vodka and anchovies.

Finally, cut the sandwiches and spread them on the mixture prepared with the anchovies, and add a spoonful of caviar.

Gently crush the sandwiches and serve.

SEA TASTE SANDWICH

for 4 people INGREDIENTS

- 8 sandwiches

- 400 g of fresh or frozen mussels

- 2 cloves of garlic - oil

- 1 sprig of parsley

- 200 g of chopped tomato pulp - salt, pepper

PREPARATION

After washing the fresh mussels, put them to cook in a pan with oil and minced garlic, stir occasionally during the cooking period. As soon as the broth starts to boil, add the parsley, salt and finally plenty of pepper and cook for about 10/15 minutes, depending on the flame.

In the meantime that the mussels are cooking, cut the sandwiches in half and remove the top, now take the tomato pulp and drain it, add oil, salt and distribute it on the sandwiches. Pepper and bake in the oven at 200 ° for about 7/8 minutes. Remove the sandwiches from the oven and add the sauce with the mussels, refit the sandwich and serve hot.

TASTY EGG SANDWICH

for 4 people INGREDIENTS

- 4 finely chopped hard-boiled eggs
- 8 slices of sandwich bread butter
- 1 teaspoon of mustard
- 1/2 teaspoon of onion powder Worcestershire sauce
- 1 tablespoon of chopped parsley
- 2 tablespoons of chopped pickled red peppers
- 2 teaspoons of vinegar
- 50 g of mayonnaise
- salt
- pepper

PREPARATION

Spread the slices of bread with butter. Take a bowl and mix the mustard, eggs, onion powder, a splash of Worcestershire sauce, pepperoni, parsley, vinegar, and mayonnaise; add salt and pepper. Divide the mixture over the four slices of bread and cover with the other slices. Take a serving dish and divide the sandwiches into triangles.

for 4 people INGREDIENTS

- 5 boiled eggs
- 8 slices of wholemeal bread
- 2 tablespoons of butter
- 1 teaspoon of curry powder
- 50 g of mayonnaise

1 teaspoon of lemon juice

1 teaspoon of Dijon mustard

salt, pepper

PREPARATION

Melt the butter in a saucepan, add the curry and cook for about a minute, stirring constantly. Let cool and add the mayonnaise, chopped eggs, lemon juice, mustard and season with a pinch of salt. Mix the mixture until smooth and spread it on the four slices of bread, close them with the other four slices and serve.

for 4 people INGREDIENTS

- 8 slices of sandwich bread

- 12 freshly toasted American peanuts

- 150 g of Roman ricotta

- 1 pinch of chili powder, salt

PREPARATION

After finely chopping the peanuts in the food processor, sift the ricotta and place it in a bowl. Add the peanuts, the pulverized chilli, a pinch of salt to the ricotta and mix the mixture well. Put the mixture in the fridge for at least 30 minutes and wait for it to thicken. Finally, take the four slices of bread and divide the mixture on them, reassemble the sandwiches and arrange them on a plate, cut them in half forming triangles and serve.

EGG AND CHIVE SANDWICH

for 4 people INGREDIENTS

- 4 hard-boiled eggs
- 3 tablespoons of chopped fresh chives
- 2 tablespoons of mayonnaise
- 6 tablespoons of butter
- 1 and 1/2 teaspoons of anchovy paste
- 8 thin slices of sliced bread - salt, pepper,
- sprigs of parsley for garnish

PREPARATION

Spread the butter with the anchovy and pepper paste just enough. With a knife chop the hard-boiled eggs and put them in a bowl together with mayonnaise, chives, salt and pepper; mix well until you get a homogeneous mixture.

Divide the sandwiches In half and spread the egg mixture on the four slices and cover with the other slices with the buttered side facing down. If you want you can also remove the crust from the bread, cut the sandwiches into triangles and arrange them on a serving dish. Before serving the sandwiches you can garnish with parsley sprigs and serve.

EGG AND BASIL SANDWICH

- for 4 people INGREDIENTS
- 8 slices of wholemeal bread
- 3 hard-boiled eggs
- 3 tablespoons of butter
- 1 tablespoon of finely chopped basil
- 4 black olives a few fillets of red pepper in oil

PREPARATION

Toast the slices of bread, in the meantime work the butter with the basil, until a homogeneous cream is obtained. As soon as the cream is ready, divide the sandwiches in half and spread it on both slices, at this point add the pitted black olives, and the pepper fillets in oil. Finally close the sandwiches with their upper part. Serve.

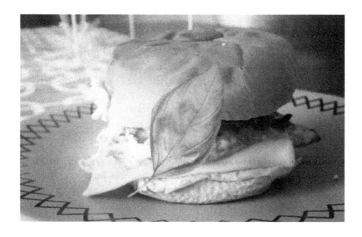

EGG AND ANCHOVIES SANDWICH

for 4 people INGREDIENTS

- 3 hard-boiled eggs
- 8 thin slices of very fresh sandwich bread
- 4 anchovy fillets
- 60 g of butter
- 1/2 teaspoon of finely chopped onion
- 1 tablespoon of mayonnaise
- 1 teaspoon of Dijon mustard
- salt and pepper
- sprigs of cress for garnish

PREPARATION

Take a bowl and put the chopped hard-boiled eggs, the chopped anchovy fillets, the butter, the onion, the mayonnaise, the mustard, a pinch of salt and pepper, now mix well until the mixture is well blended. As soon as the mixture is ready, divide the sandwiches in half and butter the inside of the upper part of the sandwiches, then spread the previously prepared mixture and close them with the other half of the sandwiches, do it with all the other sandwiches. Arrange them on a serving plate and cut them into a triangular shape. To serve.

TUNA AND MAYONNAISE SANDWICH

for 4 people INGREDIENTS

- 8 sandwiches

- 120 g of tuna in oil

- 5 tablespoons of mayonnaise sauce

- 1/2 tablespoon of chopped parsley

PREPARATION

After draining the oil from the tuna, chop it. Now cut the sandwiches in half and spread the lower part with mayonnaise, immediately afterwards lay the tuna and add the chopped parsley. Finally, cover the sandwiches with the other half and leave them to flavor for about an hour. Serve.

SANDWICH WITH BOILED FISH

for 4 people INGREDIENTS

- 8 slices of sandwich bread
- 100 g of boiled fish pulp
- 2 desalted anchovy fillets
- 50 g of butter 1 tablespoon of oil
- the juice of 1/2 lemon
- 1 teaspoon of capers - pepper

PREPARATION

Remove the bones from the anchovy fillets and season with oil, pepper, and lemon juice, then chop everything until the mixture becomes creamy. Finally, chop the capers and sprinkle them on the fish pulp. Now spread the ready mixture on the slices of bread and cover it with the top and serve.

SARDINES AND BACON SANDWICH

for 4 people INGREDIENTS

- 4 sandwiches
- 1 can of sardines
- 4 slices of smoked bacon
- 2 fresh cheese
- 1 tablespoon of capers
- 1 teaspoon of paprika
- the juice of 1 lemon
- 1 knob of butter

PREPARATION

Take a bowl, drain the sardines and add the cheeses working them with a wooden ladle, now add the chopped capers, paprika and lemon juice and mix all the ingredients well. Take the sandwiches and cut them in half, then spread the butter and fill the sandwiches with the mixture.

Take a pan and fry the bacon, then place it in the center of the sandwich. Finally close the sandwiches with the top and wrap them with aluminum foil until served.

HERRING SANDWICH

for 4 people INGREDIENTS

- 4 sandwich
- 200 g of butter
- 2 tablespoons of mustard
- 4 herring fillets

PREPARATION

Melt the butter and mix it with the mustard. Immediately after, peel the herring fillets and grill them to the right point, but do not let them dry. Then take the sandwiches, sprinkle them with mustard butter, and put the herring fillets on top. Close the sandwiches and serve.

SALMON SANDWICH

for 4 people INGREDIENTS

- 4 sandwich
- 4 slices of smoked salmon
- 100 g of canned salmon
- Worcestershire sauce
- a little broth
- the juice of 1 lemon
- mayonnaise

PREPARATION

Cut the sandwiches in half and empty the top of the crumb. Take a bowl and put the Worcestershire sauce, salmon, a little cold broth and mix everything with a blender. At the end transfer the mixture to a bowl and mix well, add the mayonnaise. After preparing the mixture, stuff the sandwiches and combine them with their upper part. To serve.

CROUTONS WITH SARDINES

for 8-9 people INGREDIENTS

- 150 g of sardines in olive oil

- 100 g of mayonnaise

- 2 teaspoons of lemon juice

- 20 g of finely chopped parsley

- Worcestershire sauce

- 18 fairly thick slices of French bread or loaf

- salt and pepper

PREPARATION

Dry the sardines and cut them into small pieces, then add the mayonnaise, Worcestershire sauce, lemon juice, salt and pepper to taste. Mix everything to get a consistent dough. Then spread all the dough on the slices of bread and bake at 200° for ten minutes or until the bread becomes crunchy. Then serve while hot.

SUMMER SANDWICH

for 4 people INGREDIENTS

- 4 slices of bread
- 1 clove of garlic
- oil
- 400 g of ripe figs
- 6 anchovy fillets in oil
- 1 fresh onion

PREPARATION

First you have to toast the bread in the oven, immediately after sprinkle it with a drizzle of oil and rub the garlic on the slice. Now peel the figs and blend them with the anchovies, as soon as the mixture is ready, add a chopped onion. Finally, distribute the mixture got on the sandwiches and serve a serving dish.

ROQUEFORT AND NUTS SANDWICH

for 4 people INGREDIENTS

- 4 sandwiches
- 400 g of Roquefort cheese
- 100 g of white cream cheese like Philadelphia
- 2 tablespoons of cognac
- 60 g of finely chopped walnuts
- 8 slices of wholemeal bread
- butter sprigs of watercress
- small cherry tomatoes

PREPARATION

Melt the white cheese, Roquefort, Cognac and chopped walnuts in a bowl, mix well with a whisk until the mixture is homogeneous. Spread over the slices of bread and cover them with the remaining slices.

Finally, the two ends of the sandwiches must be spread with butter and browned in a pan.

Arrange the sandwiches on a serving dish and cut them in half to form equal triangles. at the end garnish the sandwiches with the sprigs of watercress and cherry tomatoes.

DUTCH CHEESE SANDWICH WITH APPLES

for 4 people INGREDIENTS

- 8 slices of sandwich bread
- 4 fairly thick slices of Gouda cheese
- 1 golden apple
- 4 tablespoons of butter
- 8 teaspoons of Dijon mustard

PREPARATION

Take the bread and remove its crust, then you need to cut the Gouda into the same shape as the bread.

Take an apple and cut it into slices, the same thickness of the cheese, then take a pan and put the butter, then brown the apple for about 5 minutes, now dry the apple with absorbent paper.

Take the bread and spread the mustard adding the apple and the slices of cheese, close the sandwiches and brown the bread in a pan with the butter until the cheese has melted. Finally mash them lightly with a spatula and cut the sandwiches into triangles. Serve.

for 4 people INGREDIENTS

- 4 sandwiches
- 1 fresh goat cheese
- 80 g of Roquefort
- 2 tablespoons of cognac
- 100 g of whipping cream

PREPARATION

Take a medium-sized pan and melt the goat cheese with Roquefort and a little cognac, mix everything until you get a creamy mixture. Meanwhile, keep the sandwiches in the fridge for about half an hour. Then whip the cream and try to add it gently, mixing slowly. At the end, stuff the sandwiches and serve them.

SHRIMP SANDWICH

for 4 people INGREDIENTS

- 4 sandwich
- 1/2 onion
- 1 jar of shrimps
- 4 cheese slices
- 1 knob of butter
- 1 tablespoon of mustard

PREPARATION

Drain the prawns. Take the sandwiches and cut them in half, then spread the butter and season with a slice of cheese. Then take an onion and chop it, add some mustard and add the prawns. Cover the sandwiches with parchment paper or parchment paper and let them rest for 20 minutes until served.

for 6 people INGREDIENTS

- 150 g of well cleaned crab meat

- 6 slices of white bread

- 2 hard boiled eggs, chopped

- 50 g of mayonnaise - 6 thin slices of tomato

- 40 g of diced pickled cucumbers - 2 tablespoons of lemon juice

- 6 spoons of grated Parmesan cheese

- butter, Cayenne pepper, salt, white pepper

PREPARATION

Take a bowl and add the mayonnaise, egg, cucumber, crabmeat, lemon juice, cayenne pepper, salt and pepper to taste and mix everything until you get a creamy mixture. Meanwhile, take the slices of bread and toast them on one side only, giving them a circular shape, then spread the butter on the non-toasted side. Spread the buttered part of the bread with the mixture prepared previously, then sprinkle with a tablespoon of grated Parmesan cheese and bake at 200° for about 10 minutes, or wait for the cheese to melt. As soon as the bread is ready, garnish with thin slices of fresh tomato and serve immediately.

HOT LOBSTER CROUTONS

for 6 people INGREDIENTS

- 230 g of cooked lobster pulp cut into small pieces
- 6 large slices of white bread for sandwiches
- 1/8 liter of béchamel sauce
- 1 and 1/2 teaspoons of tomato paste
- 1 teaspoon of lemon juice
- 1 tablespoon of grated gruyere
- butter. salt and pepper

PREPARATION

Take a saucepan and thicken the béchamel, then take a bowl and put the tomato paste, the lemon juice and the béchamel itself, keep stirring until it becomes more homogeneous. Then add the lobster meat and season with salt and pepper. Now take the slices of bread and toast them on one side only. As soon as the bread is ready, try to create a disc of ten centimeters in diameter for each slice. Spread a light layer of butter on the side of the untoasted bread and add the lobster mixture, then sprinkle with the gruyere. Finally, place the croutons on the grill and cook them until the cheese melts.

My Sandwich Recipe

Title:

Servings:

_____

_____

Prep Time:

Total Time:

_____

_____

Ingredients:

_____   _____

_____   _____

_____   _____

_____   _____

_____   _____

_____   _____

My Sandwich Recipe

Title: Servings:

Prep Time: Total Time:

Ingredients:

My Sandwich Recipe

Title: Servings:

_____   _____

Prep Time: Total Time:

_____   _____

Ingredients:

_____   _____

_____   _____

_____   _____

_____   _____

_____   _____

_____   _____

My Sandwich Recipe

Title: Servings:

Prep Time: Total Time:

Ingredients:

My Sandwich Recipe

Title: Servings:

_____   _____

Prep Time: Total Time:

_____   _____

Ingredients:

_____   _____

_____   _____

_____   _____

_____   _____

_____   _____

_____   _____

My Sandwich Recipe

Title: Servings:

Prep Time: Total Time:

Ingredients:

My Sandwich Recipe

Title:

Servings:

_____

_____

Prep Time:

Total Time:

_____

_____

Ingredients:

_____

_____

_____

_____

_____

_____

_____

_____

_____

_____

My Sandwich Recipe

Title: Servings:

Prep Time: Total Time:

Ingredients:

My Sandwich Recipe

Title:

Servings:

Prep Time:

Total Time:

Ingredients:

My Sandwich Recipe

Title: Servings:

Prep Time: Total Time:

Ingredients:

My Sandwich Recipe

Title: Servings:

_____   _____

Prep Time: Total Time:

_____   _____

Ingredients:

_____   _____

_____   _____

_____   _____

_____   _____

_____   _____

_____   _____

My Sandwich Recipe

Title: Servings:

Prep Time: Total Time:

Ingredients:

My Sandwich Recipe

Title: Servings:

_____   _____

Prep Time: Total Time:

_____   _____

Ingredients:

_____   _____

_____   _____

_____   _____

_____   _____

_____   _____

_____   _____

CPSIA information can be obtained
at www.ICGtesting.com
Printed in the USA
BVHW061250020621
608627BV00008B/709